ALL THINGS PANDAS FOR KIDS

FILLED WITH PLENTY OF FACTS, PHOTOS, AND FUN TO LEARN ALL ABOUT PANDAS

ANIMAL READS

THIS BOOK BELONGS TO...

_____

_____

WWW.ANIMALREADS.COM

CONTENTS

Hello Pandas!	1
What Is a Panda?	5
Meet The Giant Panda	11
Meet The Red Panda	17
The History of the Panda's	25
Characteristics and Appearance	35
The Life Cycle of Pandas	55
More Awesome Panda Facts	63
Help Pandas Survive	67
Thank You!	71

HELLO PANDAS!
WELCOME TO THE EXCITING WORLD OF PANDAS...

Can you think of a more adorable animal than a panda?

We bet you'd have a hard time naming one. After all, few animals are known for being so insanely, *ridiculously,* cute.

Aside from their clownish antics, super-round bodies, squeezable cheeks, and sweet eyes, pandas are also famous for being one of the most **vulnerable** animals on earth. Only a few remain in the wild, although many live and thrive in dedicated research centers in their native China. Many organizations are fighting to keep the animals thriving, and they are winning the fight! After a 30-year mission to double the number of pandas in the wild, China declared they are no longer endangered but vulnerable.

Mind you...we bet you're only thinking of the black-and-white panda species...*areweright*?

The **Giant Panda**, as the teddy bear-like creature is known, is the one most people envision when they hear the word 'panda.' *But did you know that there is another species of panda?*

That's right!

If you're an avid panda lover, you may already know there are two panda species on our planet. If not... you are about to meet the **red panda**, the lesser-known but equally enchanting cousin of the Giant.

Ready to discover more about these incredible animals?

Then join us as we dive into the wonderful world of pandas, the world's most adored bears!

WHAT DID ONE PANDA SAY TO THE OTHER?

You're being un**BEAR**able!

WHAT IS A PANDA?

It probably won't come as much of a surprise, but pandas are a member of the **Ursidae** family of animals. Or, in other words, they are a type of **bear**.

FUN FACT: What *is* surprising is the fact that this has only been confirmed recently. For many years, experts were at odds because the panda – often called panda bear – shared many features with both bears *and* raccoons. *Weird, right?* But it actually isn't, given raccoons and bears do share a common ancestor. This means that somewhere along the line of evolution, millions of years ago, both species of animals came from the same ancient creature.

Anywho, experts were divided as to which side of the ancient creature's family pandas derive, and the mystery was only solved recently, thanks to molecular studies. So now it's official: **pandas ARE bears!**

Giant pandas and red pandas are the only two recognized panda species in the world, although they are only mildly related. They may have also originated from the same bear-like ancestor. Yet, these two very distant cousins are only *somewhat* alike.

Want to hear another shocker? Scientists spent years debating whether giant and red pandas could even be classified as two species of the same animal. *Yes, we know, what's new?* Scientists might seem to argue a lot, but it's all part of their job – experts in their field continuously test each other's findings and theories, but they all share a common goal: **to find answers to some of the most puzzling questions about our planet, all the creatures in it, and beyond!**

If you're familiar with pandas, you might know that size, and color, are the most obvious ways the Giant and red pandas differ.

But there's more!

Keen to find out what?

You know what to do!

MEET THE GIANT PANDA

P o....is that you?

Oh, a *Kung Fu Panda* indeed!

Giant pandas are big, fuzzy creatures with black and white fur. They have black ears, a white face, and black circles around their eyes. They look like bears wearing sunglasses, but they're not. Giant pandas can't **really** do kung fu either, but they still look pretty cool!

One thing you'll notice about the giant panda is its size. After all, it's in the name! Its bulky body looks so huggable. No wonder you see a lot of panda stuffed toys around. You might even have one of Po in your room!

Male pandas can grow up to **5 feet tall**, about the height of a medium Christmas tree or an average human. Female giant pandas are usually a little bit smaller.

Since they're *so* big, giant pandas can be pretty heavy. They can weigh up to about **220 pounds** or 100 kilograms. That's about as heavy as a two-door refrigerator!

Most people assume giant pandas are herbivores because all they seem to be doing is chewing bamboo. In reality, however, they are what's called **herbivorous carnivorans**. This means they *can* eat meat, but they don't do it often.

They'd much prefer to eat juicy bamboo all day long. Crazy to know one could get that big eating bamboo and vegetables – *guess you might also want to eat more veggies to grow big and strong, right?*

Despite their overwhelming size, there's nothing about the giant panda that makes it seem dangerous and aggressive. Quite the opposite, this is one of the world's most docile and gentle giants, and it's partly why they haven't fared so well in the wild.

Giant pandas can live for around 20 years in the wild. **Less than 2,000 individuals remain**, living at high altitudes in the wild temperate forests of southwestern China. Another 600 are protected in zoos and sanctuaries in China and at least a dozen other countries.

WHY DO PANDA BEARS HAVE A HAIRY COAT?

FUR protection!

MEET THE RED PANDA

Scientists call this the lesser panda, but the adorable rust-colored bear is better known as the red panda.

Red pandas are all the rage right now, thanks to the recently released Disney-Pixar movie, *Turning Red*, starring Meilin, who turns into a red panda whenever she gets too excited!

We're happy to see the red panda finally achieve some worldwide attention. Its black-and-white cousin usually steals the limelight, and this gorgeous little guy is often forgotten.

Red pandas don't look much like giant pandas. Firstly, because they are much smaller and, secondly, because they have reddish-brown fur with a black underside. Red pandas also have a gloriously bushy tail, which giant pandas lack.

At first sight, you might not think they are related to giant pandas at all, and that's *precisely* what has scientists a little undecided. Red pandas have a lovable and rather distinctive white face. To many, they look like raccoons or even the baby of a fox and cat.

Red pandas grow to just about **20 to 26 inches long** (not including their beautiful tail) and weigh around **9 pounds** on average. That's about the weight of a one-month-old baby or a 22-inch LED TV!

Like giant pandas, red pandas are considered **herbivorous carnivorans**. They also prefer eating bamboo or other fruits and veggies instead of meat.

Unlike the gentle giant panda, the red panda looks quite fierce. *Just between us, it's only in appearance.* The fur markings on their faces often make them look angry, as if they're constantly frowning.

Then again, you'd probably frown too, if you were classified as a **vulnerable** species. *This means red pandas are in danger of going extinct or dying out in the wild.*

Red pandas may not be naturally aggressive, but this is a creature that's certainly ready to fend off predators. If threatened, provoked, or frightened, it will lash out.

Red pandas don't have many relatives at all in the animal world, and even its closest is the very distant giant panda. To solve the issue of classifying this animal, experts came to a wonderful compromise: *red pandas would be given their own unique classification!*

The red panda is now the only member of the **Ailuridae** family.

Can you imagine being the sole member of your own unique family? That's pretty amazing, isn't it?

Red pandas are also divided into two subspecies: the **Himalayan red panda** and the **Chinese red**

panda. These two species differ in more than the name and actually showcase distinct DNA or the molecules that make up their bodies. That's the reason scientists have to classify them as two different subspecies.

In the wild, red pandas live for about 10 years. **Only 10,000 individuals remain** in the mountain regions of China, India, Myanmar, Nepal, and Bhutan.

Unfortunately, both giant pandas and red pandas are vulnerable species. Nobody knows for sure just how many giant pandas and red pandas walked the earth before humans evolved enough to start clearing forests to build cities and highways. But we bet there were many more than there are today.

FUN FACT: The panda originated in China, and it is here that most of them still live. Out of all the captive pandas, those residing in zoos and sanctuaries, only **49** are found outside of China.

THE HISTORY OF THE PANDA'S
THEIR EVOLUTION

Now, you might be wondering, how long have pandas been around? Pretty long, actually. Both giant pandas and red pandas have been around for over three to five *MILLION* years!

Not much is known of the modern panda's history. The closest ancestor discovered was the *Ailuropoda baconi*, a small bear-like animal that lived in China about 750,000 years ago. The thick and luscious forests of China have not revealed many *fossils* to help scientists unravel the mystery of the panda's lineage.

Fossils are remains of skeletons embedded in the earth for millions of years. Scientists continually find fossils of prehistoric animals, which is how they can create a timeline of their evolution.

WHY ARE PANDAS ENDANGERED?

There are a few reasons why the panda population is so low. For one thing, pandas used to be hunted. In ancient China, people believed that panda fur could protect them from evil spirits. Some even made talismans out of them. Talismans are items believed to ward off bad luck, so they are used as good-luck charms.

Of course, panda fur isn't and never was magical but ancient cultures were very superstitious and believed in all sorts of magic.

The good news is that hunting pandas is no longer allowed. In fact, the panda is a revered national treasure in China, and several policies are in place to ensure pandas are taken care of. Yet many scientists say the past has caused *irrevocable* damage, meaning we can't undo the damage that's been done.

What's more, hunting has been replaced with *deforestation*, the practice of chopping down a forest to make room for people or to utilize wood for building material.

The panda is still in danger of losing its home, and life, due to forest harvesting.

Like many wildlife species, pandas cannot simply '*move*' to greener pastures. These are highly localized animals that thrive in specific forests and eat specific food. They have nowhere else to go if we cut down their natural habitat.

WHERE DO PANDAS LIVE?

Speaking of forests, giant pandas and red pandas live in bamboo forests at high altitudes. But you won't find them living in the same place.

The giant panda prefers to live in humid mountainous forests about 4,000 - 10,000 feet above sea level.

Can you imagine living thousands of feet above the sea?

Giant pandas live in one region of China, although, once upon a time, they used to have more habitats. Aside from the southwestern corner of the country, giant pandas were also found in the central, southern, and eastern parts of China. They also used to live in neighboring countries, like Myanmar and northern Vietnam.

These days though, most giant pandas are found only in 20 isolated areas in western China. These areas are located in the Sichuan, Gansu, and Shaanxi provinces. Sichuan province is considered the main habitat of giant pandas. It even earned the nickname *"home of giant pandas."*

On the other hand, Red pandas live in the thick bamboo forests of the Himalayas. You can also find them in the adjacent areas of eastern Asia.

It might be cool to get a map and pin these amazing places. If you are ever lucky enough to travel to China to meet pandas, you'll know where to go!

Red pandas are a little hardier than giant pandas and can live at even higher altitudes. They're most active and energetic when there's snow and prefer temperatures between 50 and 77 degrees Fahrenheit (or 10-25 degrees Celsius).

Like giant pandas, red pandas also live some 6,000 to 12,000 feet above sea level. After all, the

Himalayas are a pretty high mountain range! One of its peaks is actually Mount Everest.

That's the tallest mountain on the entire planet.

WHAT GOES BLACK, WHITE, BLACK, WHITE, BLACK, WHITE?

A giant panda rolling down a hill!

CHARACTERISTICS AND APPEARANCE

More than just huggable-looking bears, pandas have several unique features. From their physical characteristics to their diet, let's take a look at what makes pandas awesome creatures!

PHYSICAL APPEARANCE

Panda fur might look plush and soft, but it's not just for show. No matter the color, all panda fur is there to keep the animal warm and to help it blend in with its surrounding landscape. Giant pandas cleverly camouflage against a snowy backdrop, whereas red pandas are darker, so they are better at absorbing heat from the sun. Given they live at higher altitudes, this is a really important trait. What's more, red pandas like to live in forests where red is a more common color.

FUN FACT: An ancient Chinese legend says that giant pandas were once all-white bears. One day, a panda cub was about to be attacked by a leopard, but a young girl sacrificed her life to save it. When pandas came to her funeral, they rubbed their paws on the ashes from a fire. As they were grieving for the girl, they wiped their tears and hugged each other. This is how pandas got their black fur.

Would you believe us if we told you that pandas are excellent climbers?

Videos of pandas falling off perches and trees are commonplace on the internet, and they make for entertaining viewing. **In reality, these big fuzzy bears can scale great heights even if they look totally clumsy.** It's all thanks to their paws, which have five fingers and an extra thumb. This thumb is actually an enlarged wrist bone and is what allows them to have a good grip on things.

This thumb is especially helpful when they're holding bamboo to eat.

Giant pandas also have rear paws that point inward. **It's why they look like they're waddling when they walk!** Unlike some animals that move on all fours, giant pandas can easily stand on their hind legs. They can even roll, somersault, and bathe in the dust or snow. Much like other bears, giant pandas are also able swimmers.

Red pandas are just as skilled as giant pandas when it comes to climbing. In fact, red pandas spend most of their time on top of trees and can even swing through them! Their sharp claws and hairy soles allow them to have a good grip on tree trunks and branches.

Red pandas can move quickly thanks to their flexible ankles. The way their leg bones are positioned helps them make quick movements. They can even climb down tree trunks head-first!

Compared to giant pandas, red pandas look like they have more balance. It's all because of their long, bushy tails.

Their tails keep them steady while walking and climbing and protect them from the cold, strong winds, and harsh weather. Since they love the snow, red pandas don't hibernate during winter. While sleeping, their tails curl around their bodies to keep them cozy.

Last but certainly not least is the giant panda's mouth. If you've ever seen bamboo, you might know that this is a very tough plant. Luckily, the giant panda has strong jaws and large molar teeth. This helps them strip and chew bamboo.

EATING AND DIET

If there's one thing that giant pandas and red pandas have in common, it's that they both eat bamboo. In fact, the word panda comes from the Nepalese word "*ponya*," which means bamboo. This explains why giant pandas and red pandas have the same name, even if they aren't really related.

Pandas love bamboo *so* much that they can, quite literally, live on the stuff. It is almost *all* they eat. Giant pandas can eat nearly 80 pounds or 36.4 kilograms of bamboo each day.

Now that's *A LOT* of bamboo!

If easy to find, giant pandas are also happy munching on eggs, fish, and honey, as well as fruit.

Unlike their cousins in the wild, giant pandas that live in zoos don't always get to eat bamboo. To keep them healthy, zookeepers might feed them milk, cereals, and fresh fruits and vegetables from the garden.

If food is really hard to come by, wild giant pandas might sometimes eat small animals like rodents. Their digestive system is all set up to eat meat, but they still prefer bamboo when given the choice. *So why are they even carnivorous, you might ask?* Experts believe that the panda's ancestors were dedicated meat-eaters, and they have inherited the trait despite changing their diet habits throughout their evolution.

FUN FACT: A truly puzzling thing is that although pandas love to eat bamboo, they actually can't digest *cellulose*, which is the main component of bamboo! Because of this, giant pandas have to go to the bathroom as much as 50 times a day (***ooooh boy***) and spend about 16 hours of their day eating. No wonder, cellulose goes straight through them, so no matter how much bamboo they eat, they're constantly hungry!

Red pandas are similar and also have the digestive system of a carnivore, but their diet is 95% bamboo. Since they don't have the giant panda's big, strong jaws and teeth, they only eat the leafy tips of bamboo. They can also eat the tender shoots, but they avoid the hard, woody stems.

Insects, grass, roots, and grubs also feature on the red panda's daily menu, making up about 5% of their overall diet. Naturally, they can also eat fresh veggies and fruits and, on occasion, have been known to hunt small mammals and birds.

What's your favorite fresh food to eat? Is it something you could share with a panda?

COMMUNICATION

One of the first things you might have learned about animals is what they sound like. Dogs bark, cats meow, and birds chirp. **However, not**

all animals communicate by making sounds. Pandas are one of those animals.

For the giant panda, communication happens through scent marking. This means they leave their smell on trees, rocks, or even the ground. By rubbing their scent on these places and paths, giant pandas can convey different messages. A particular scent can let other giant pandas know if there's danger ahead. Another kind of scent might tell other giant pandas if they need to group together or separate. Other times, it just tells them if another giant panda is nearby.

Smelly messages? You bet!

The scent of giant pandas can also drive intruders away from their homes. When other animals smell an unfamiliar scent, they usually interpret it as a sign of danger and stay well clear of the area.

FUN FACT: During mating season, male and female giant pandas also use their scent to find a partner. Female giant pandas are likely to mate with a male whose scent they already know.

Now, you might be wondering if giant pandas *can* make sounds. They can! But they don't always use their voice to communicate. They sometimes vocalize when playing and mating but rarely do this when communicating with others of their kind.

Unlike other animals, giant pandas also don't have visual signals. You can say that their faces aren't very expressive. Their tails are stubs, so they can't exactly wag them around as cats or dogs do. Their ears can't perk up or curl down, they don't have crests or manes, and their fur doesn't bristle when angry or scared. This means they lack in body language. *Their body parts aren't able to express their mood.*

If you really think about it, it's a little bit strange that giant pandas don't communicate as other animals do. But since they like living alone, this kind of makes sense. Pandas are **solitary** animals and only come together to mate. They wouldn't have use for visual signals if they usually don't have other giant pandas to talk to!

You might think that it's a little bit sad that giant pandas tend to live alone, but this isn't necessarily a bad thing. Animals like giant pandas are happy to keep to themselves. I guess you can say they just really enjoy their own company. Typically, all bears are solitary animals, and you will only ever find them in multiples when mating or when a female is raising young cubs.

As for the red panda, communication is the same, with some slight differences. Red pandas also rely on scent-marking to communicate, and they do this by rubbing the base of their tails against a surface. They might also pee on a particular spot. When marking their territory, they use the scent glands between their footpads to leave their smell.

If you ever see a red panda doing some kind of cute wiggle dance, rest assured it is only scent marking.

FUN FACT: Believe it or not, humans can't actually smell the scent of pandas. Only pandas and other animals can! When red pandas come across an unfamiliar scent, they use their tongues to figure out this new smell. They do this via a cone-like structure on their tongue that catches tiny droplets of liquid from new scents. This cone then transfers the liquid into a special gland inside their mouth. This gland is what red pandas use to interpret the scent. That's a very complex way of smelling the world!

Like giant pandas, red pandas can also vocalize from time to time. They can make sounds like hissing, grunting, squealing, and even twittering. Young red panda cubs make high-pitched noises when they feel threatened or distressed. It's their way of letting their parents know that they don't feel safe and are scared.

How do you express your different moods?

ACTIVITIES AND BEHAVIOR

Pandas spend a lot of the day sleeping. Giant pandas, in particular, *love* to sleep. They take naps that can last around two to four hours after every feed. And that's a lot of naps considering they spend 16 hours of the day eating!

Have you ever felt sleepy whenever you're full?

When giant pandas sleep, they lie on their side, back, or belly. They even sleep while curled up or sprawled on the ground.

Sometimes, they enjoy sleeping so much that some naps can last around six hours or more. This often happens during the summer months. It's probably because the weather is warmer, so they sleep better.

Now here's a doozy: *pandas need to poop so often that they can even do it while sleeping. Their digestive systems work non-stop to process bamboo cellulose, and it certainly doesn't stop*

when the panda sleeps. It just keeps going and going!

While giant pandas often live alone, they can sometimes form groups over larger areas. Some panda territories can have seven to 15 giant pandas living harmoniously. Still, they tend to avoid socializing with other giant pandas. They might be friendly and non-aggressive animals, but they sure like to keep to themselves.

When it comes to their sleeping habits, red pandas are **crepuscular**. This means they're most active during dawn and dusk. As for the rest of the day, they spend it conserving their energy. This is because bamboo doesn't give them a lot of nutrients.

THE LIFE CYCLE OF PANDAS

NEWBORNS

Both giant pandas and red pandas have their breeding season during the northern summer. Most babies are born usually sometime in August.

Compared to human moms, panda moms have shorter pregnancies, usually lasting 90 to 160 days. That's around three to five months that they carry their babies in their tummies. Human moms carry babies for much longer, which is around nine months.

Giant panda females usually give birth to one or two babies. Sometimes, they select the strongest cub and care only for that one. It's one of the reasons they don't have such a big population. Giant panda dads aren't involved in caring for babies at all.

You'll be surprised to know that newborn giant pandas are super tiny! They only weigh about 100 grams or 4 ounces. They're also only 5 inches long. You can say that they're only as long as two adult thumbs and as heavy as a small box of paper clips!

Newborn giant pandas are pink because they don't have much fur yet. They're blind and fully dependent on their mothers. When they grow a bit of hair, it's all white at first. They don't grow their black fur until they're about a month old.

On the other hand, red pandas are covered in fur when they're born. This is to protect them from the cold weather. Red panda babies are also really tiny, more or less the same size as giant panda cubs.

As opposed to the giants, though, a red panda can give birth to around one to four cubs.

When giant pandas are born, mothers stay in the den for the first three months. They don't leave to eat or drink and are solely concerned with caring for their cubs.

When a pregnant red panda female is looking to nest, she will search for hollow tree trunks, stumps, or tree holes. She may even use rocks to build a suitable birth den and then line it with leaves, moss, or any other soft plant.

CUBS

After around six to eight weeks, giant panda babies start opening their eyes. They can't move around much until they're about eight to nine months old, which is when they are finally fully weaned off their mother's milk.

Red panda cubs grow up much faster and only stay in the nest for about 90 days. After that, they stay with their mother until the next summer. That's when another breeding season starts.

YOUNG ADULTS

Giant panda cubs reach their "teenage" years at two years old. That's about the time they leave their moms. At this age, they've grown to about 220 pounds (100 kilograms) or their normal size.

Red panda cubs leave their moms much earlier. They do this when they turn one year old.

To humans, that might sound super young. But, to pandas, that's just about the right age. After all, they have a shorter lifespan. It's why they mature faster.

MATURITY

Giant pandas are considered adults at around four to six years old. This means they can have their own families when breeding season comes. Red pandas, on the other hand, are considered full-grown adults at the age of two.

PANDA-MONIUM!

MORE AWESOME PANDA FACTS

We hope you've enjoyed learning more about the fascinating pandas. But we're not done yet! Here are some more awesome panda facts we know you will love:

DID YOU KNOW?

- The eyes of a giant panda aren't like the eyes of normal bears. They're actually vertical slits! They look more like the eyes of a cat.

- Giant panda cubs are pretty brave. They practice climbing trees as early as five months old!

- Red pandas were named 'pandas' about 50 years before the giant kind also received the same name.

- They might look big and lumbering, but giant pandas can actually do handstands. They climb a tree backward until they stand on their hands. Why on earth would they ever need to do this? To leave their scent higher up on a tree trunk, of course!

- Thanks to their curved claws, red pandas can rotate 180 degrees while on tree bark!

- They might move on all fours but don't make a red panda angry! They will stand on their hind legs when they feel threatened or provoked.

- There is an International Red Panda Day! This has been celebrated every third Saturday of September since 2010. The event helps raise public awareness about red pandas so they can be protected and preserved forever.

HELP PANDAS SURVIVE

Pandas are beautiful creatures that deserve our protection. While they aren't classified as endangered anymore, they're still a vulnerable species. With some help, the panda population might one day be restored.

Some ways you can help pandas survive is by supporting organizations like the **World Wildlife Fund (WWF)**. The WWF is a non-governmental organization that advocates for the preservation of pandas and their habitats. They work together with other groups, like the Chinese government, so pandas stay protected.

You can also learn more about threats to pandas, such as deforestation and habitat loss. Together with your parents, you can spread awareness on social media about the dangers pandas face. Through this, you can use your voice to help stop practices that endanger these wonderful animals.

Symbolically "*adopting*" pandas is also one way you can help. Zoos and other organizations allow you to "*adopt*" pandas for a small fee. Think of this more as a donation than actually adopting a panda.

By working together and spreading the word, we can share the beauty of the earth with pandas for a long, long time.

HAVE A

PANDASTIC

DAY!

THANK YOU!

Thank you for reading this book and for allowing us to share our love for pandas with you!

If you've enjoyed this book, please let us know by leaving a rating and a brief review wherever you made your purchase! This helps us spread the word to other readers!

Thank you for your time, and have an awesome day!

For more information, please visit:

www.animalreads.com

© Copyright 2022 - All rights reserved Admore Publishing

ISBN: 978-3-96772-133-1

ISBN: 978-3-96772-134-8

Animal Reads at www.animalreads.com

The content contained within this book may not be reproduced, duplicated or transmitted without direct written permission from the author or the publisher.

Under no circumstances will any blame or legal responsibility be held against the publisher, or author, for any damages, reparation, or monetary loss due to the information contained within this book. Either directly or indirectly.

Published by Admore Publishing: Gotenstraße, Berlin, Germany

www.admorepublishing.com

www.ingramcontent.com/pod-product-compliance
Lightning Source LLC
LaVergne TN
LVHW020141080526
838202LV00048B/3987